A Village of Verse

A Village of Verse

Edited by

Norman Watson

First published in Great Britain in 2001 by
Bagillt Heritage Society

Castle Villa
High Street Bagillt
Flintshire CH6 6HE
Telephone (01352) 712558

www.bagillt.org.uk

© Copyright 2001 Copyright Contributors

Printed by:
ProPrint
Riverside Cottage
Great North Road
Stibbington
Peterborough PE8 6LR

ISBN: 0 9540868 0 5

This Book is dedicated
to
Ceridwen Eluned Meese (Ceri)

Who planted the seed

ACKNOWLEDGEMENTS

Illustrations
by
Brenda Bruce

Front Cover. 'The Holy' (Deebank Dock)
by
Jim Dinsdale-Potter

FOREWORD

I cannot remember the last time I was in Bagillt. I used to drive through it to get to Flint, to Chester, to Liverpool, to London. Now there's a by-pass past the by-pass. I went for tea there after school, to my friend John Doleman. I bought my first car there from Harry Davies. A turquoise morris minor convertible with a white hood. Shades of Hollywood even then! And I went to the Regent Cinema - although I never played Bingo there.

But, for me Bagillt is special. My father Isaac was born and grew up there. He went down the colliery at Bettwsfield aged 14, and spent his shifts up to his chest in water, hacking out the coal. All his life he bore the bruises on his back from a pit fall. He escaped all this by marrying my mother, Margaret, a beauty from Flint and together they opened a shop in Bryn Celyn.

Still, Bagillt became the place I passed through. Never stopping. Never thinking of its past, its people. Never imagining its poetry.

But the following pages are a revelation. A hundred or so poems from people of all backgrounds, ages and experiences. Poems of hope and anger - of bitter personal experience and of love and joy. Wistful poems for a way of life that has gone and words of optimism for the future. War poems containing images and thoughts that the author has carried for years *contrast with the bright words of school children.*

I thank the people of Bagillt for this chance to share their poetry with all of us.

Jonathan Pryce.

PREFACE

Our village is so full of talent
As this book of verse will portray
The poets have sent out a message
In their own individual way
Many reflect on the good things
And also the bad times in life
Days they don't want to remember
Surrounded by trouble and strife
Created by few for so many
Enjoy every word that you read
It comes out of the heart I can promise
From a very emotional breed.

Brian Doleman

CONTENTS

Reflection	William Harris	1
Bagillt	Vince Jones	2
Baby Smiles	Vince Jones	3
Who Can Tell	Vince Jones	4
Are We Friends	Vince Jones	5
Tranquility	Ceri Meese	6
The Pentre	Clydwyn A Green	8
Now And Then	Brian Doleman	10
Rose Place	Brian Doleman	11
On The Ebb	Brian Doleman	12
Walk A Mile In My Shoes	Glenys Humphreys	14
Summer Storm	Glenys Humphreys	15
Feelings	Glenys Humphreys	16
My River	Glenys Humphreys	17
A Round Remembered	Kath Williams	18
Fachwen	Kath Williams	20
William Richard Totty	Norman Watson	21
Our Street	Norman Watson	22
Bagillt On Dee	Norman Watson	24
Progress	Norman Watson	26
Coed Bagillt	Norman Watson	27
Oh I Do Like To Be . . .	Joan Hough	28
Dissolutionment	Joan Hough	30
Love Is . . .	Joan Hough	31
Life And Death	David Watson	32
Regeneration	Nigel Ward Renshaw	33
Two 'Haiku' Poems	Jacqueline Wilson	34
To A Grieving Mother	Jacqueline Wilson	35
The Lady In The Window	Jacqueline Wilson	36
Desecration	Jacqueline Wilson	37
Betrayal	Jacqueline Wilson	38
Contrasts	Eryl Margaret	39
A Moment	Eryl Margaret	40
Fishy Nonsense	Eryl Margaret	41
Hen Ardal Bagillt	George Tattum	42
Cymru	Samuel M Hughes	44

Cadi Ha	Traditional	45
Mrs Ellen Hughes	Norman Closs Parry	46
Thomas Pennant	Norman Closs Parry	46
Ngh'lennig	Traditional	48
Y Dawnsio Haf	Traditional	48
The Book Of Life	Anni Watson	49
My Nain	Rhiannon Bennett	50
School Song	Jessica Roberts	51
Land Of My Fathers	Sarah Pugh & Rebecca Jordan	52
The Hedgehog	Sophie Williams	53
The Eclipse	Katy James	54
Spring	Jade Jones	55
Sports Day	Amy Horne	56
Tomatoes	Thomas Roberts	57
Bumpy Lumps	Carla Owen	58
Why?	Caroline Evans	59
The Haunted House	Stephanie Wright	60
Quiet	John Ovens	61
Home For Retired Gentlefolk	John Ovens	62
August Eighty-One	John Ovens	64
Food For Thought	John Ovens	65
My Friend	Pamela Watson	66
The Dee Horizon	Danielle Rush	67
The Communal Heart	Danielle Rush	68
Just Asking	Vince Jones	69
Bergen Belsen	Vince Jones	70
A Letter Home	Vince Jones	71
Just Out Of Sight	Vince Jones	73
Innerness	Vince Jones	74
Life's Cycle	Ceri Meese	75
My Granda	Ceri Meese	76
My Chosen Road	Ceri Meese	78
Trust?	Barry Doleman	80
Ode To Barrymore	Barry Doleman	81
My Shadow	Bridey Watson	82

Bagillt Reflections	Brian Doleman	84
Before My Time	Brian Doleman	85
Old Bagillt Station	Brian Doleman	86
The 'Park'	Brian Doleman	87
The Arms Of Cwm Pennant	Norman Watson	88
The Burning Ash Of Broadoaks Wood	Norman Watson	89
Autumn Love	Norman Watson	90
The Owl	Glenys Humphreys	92
Ebb And Flow	Glenys Humphreys	93
Caterwauling	Glenys Humphreys	94
Two Ounces Of Dolly Mixtures	Joan Hough	95
The Veggie Party	Joan Hough	96
A Mist	Joan Hough	98
Happy Days	Brian Doleman	99
The 'Holy Waters'	Brian Doleman	100
The Curse	Brian Doleman	101
'Tufty'	Brian Doleman	102
The Antiques Roadshow	Norman Watson	104
Roadshow Blues	Liz Potter	106
The Family Tree	Norman Watson	108
Four Women. Their Strengths	Eryl Margaret	109
Shadows In The Light	Eryl Margaret	110
It's Tuesday	Eryl Margaret	111
The Last Parade	Vince Jones	112
Wales	Vince Jones	114
After The Strike	John Ovens	116
Stretching	John Ovens	117
The Greater Friend	William Harris	118
Memory Garden	William Harris	119

REFLECTION

Sweet love you like unto a rose
Undaunted slowly swaying.
At eventide when petals close
As if so proudly praying.
With petals pointed to the sky
Covered by the dew,
As tears from a lover's eyes
When love has proved untrue.

Love, as a rose, must surely flower
Beauty amid the thorn,
The truest heart, love may devour
Yet leave it so forlorn.
And yet to think true love and hate
Akin as all things living,
To hurt, a thorn won't hesitate
While hearts may try forgiving.

William Harris

BAGILLT

So silent now this place once filled with noise,
Belching chimneys now removed
No more the clog shod boys.
Docks and lead works now the distant past
Plundered coal seams costing blood,
Like the Miners, did not last.
Riches made by heartless owners, who
With pittance, hardship, they called pay
To the men who went to hew.

Gone the characters, and village shop with 'tick',
Singing voices seldom heard.
No more the Bobby's stick.
A modern village, foundations built on pride.
New bricks and tile cannot erase
Where old Bagillt died.

Vince Jones

BABY SMILES

No sunshine ever half as bright
Though set against a cloudless sky.
No grass so fresh though pearled with dew,
I could not give the reason why.

No sunrise or yet sun that sets
Can form a picture of such charm.
No softened shapes by winter's snow
All gentle curves that show no harm.

The laughing stream amid the rocks
Could calm the wind and please the eye.
No singing bird at early dawn
To welcome yet another day.

All these things we know and love
And seldom will our minds beguile,
But mediocre when compared
To what we see in baby smiles.

Vince Jones

WHO CAN TELL

How can you tell when a little fish sighs
When it swims around in a tank.
How can you tell when a little fish smiles
When its face is always blank.
Maybe its mamma sees these things
And knows just what to do
But can she tell when a little fish cries
I'm sure she can. Can you?

How can you tell when a rose is sad
In a garden full of flowers.
How can you tell when a rose is glad
As it climbs along the bowers.
Perhaps a bee can answer this
If only it could say,
But who can understand the bee
We can't, but another bee may.

Vince Jones

ARE WE FRIENDS

Side by side they lay
Like lovers on a grassy bank.
An arm across a naked shoulder lay
A hand, gripped upon a youthful flank.
Their calm young faces unsmiling, very near
Hold each other's eyes, now blind.

Tommy Khaki, Jerry Grey, means nothing here.
They were young and dead, one fear, one kind.
Did they help each other
With last and final breath,
Make amends, their quarrel done?
They go together, into death.

Vince Jones (Belgium 1945)

TRANQUILITY

I came upon a rustic bridge
That spanned a tumbling stream.
I slowly walked across the planks
And soon began to dream.
I looked down upon the rippling stream
Splashing its way as if unseen.
Beneath, lay pebbles clear and bright
With tadpoles scurrying in delight.

A twig floats by beneath the bridge
My attention promptly drew,
I follow it on its merry way
And watch it float from view.
Twig, I wonder where you will rest
As you sail this rivulet.
Will you reach the open sea
Or snuggle 'neath an overhanging tree.

As you disappear from view
You rouse me from my reveries.
Whereupon I made a vow
To treasure all such memories.

Ceri Meese

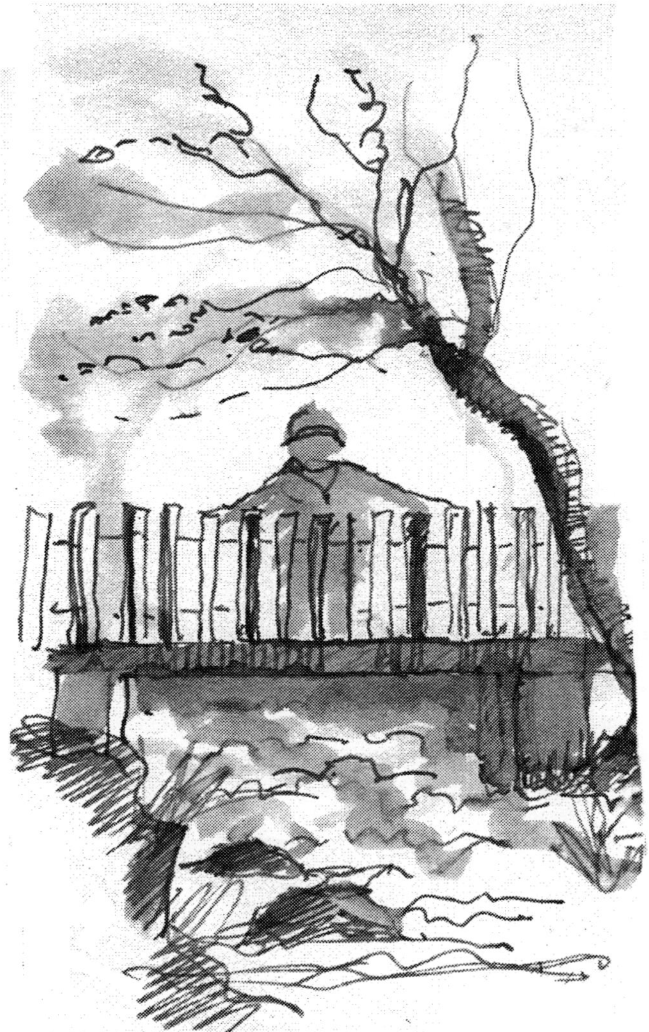

THE PENTRE

I was born in a village called Bagillt
In a house down old Station Road.
Right opposite the old Cambrian Brewery
Just the other side of the road.
At the bottom of the street a pub called The Dee,
At the top a pub called The Stag,
And we all lived in the middle
So life was never a drag.

We never had a toilet or bathroom
In them days they cost a few bob.
So we all did the best we could
We just went down on the 'Cob'.
In those days the Cob was a gold mine
The salmon and fluke were divine.
But you can't live like that these days
You'd definitely end up with a fine.

Now coal was never a problem
As there was a coal mine close by,
Our fires always burnt brightly,
As bright as the sun in the sky.
Now carnivals were always a highlight
We all got dressed up and took part.
But the star of the show was the Queen of May
On the back of the old horse and cart.

Then the war came along, the fun ended
And most of the boys went away.
They all went quite willing,
While hoping to come back someday.
I was one of the lucky ones
And came back home one day.
I took one look at the village,
And vowed that I'd never stray.

I'm still here to this present day
Glad and happy I decided to stay,
I'm somewhat older now and a little grey
But that's life, at the end of the day.

Clydwyn A Green

NOW AND THEN

From only just a child of ten
Once a year I stood with men,
Who thought so much about the past
They hoped the peace would surely last.
The ones who gave the most away
Are etched upon that stone today.

Who goes now, that went before
Very few, the truth for sure.
Perhaps these days there is no gain
For standing smartly in the rain,
The chosen few who sing and pray
Will honour their Remembrance Day.

Brian Doleman

ROSE PLACE

Mrs Price at number one
Agnes Allsopp just next door,
The Williams in number three
With the Prices again at four
Number five was John Y Bont
Mrs Renshaw number six.
All the doors were open then
So everyone could mix.
The Pierces and the Simons
At seven and eight were fine
And on the end was Mrs Hughes
Who lived at number nine.

Brian Doleman

ON THE EBB

The fishing in our village
Is a heritage for me,
By the quiet restless waters
Of the flowing River Dee.
Well marked to show its sandy hills
The channels and the Salmon kills.

Early in the morning
Before the dawn has landed,
The vessels shed their anchor ropes
From bows the mud has branded.
Then slowly drift into the tide
With crews half drunk and starry-eyed.

Coffee black has almost gone
A coloured sky that marks the dawn,
Flocks of Curlew on the wing,
Whimbrel, Peewit start to sing.
The men alert with oar each side
Prepare to fight an ebbing tide.

These fish a quarry they must stalk
Armed with nylon lead and cork.
The net must drop, the time precise
Or alas the catch will not suffice
To feed a family wife and hound
Or sell at ninety pence a pound.

Brian Doleman

WALK A MILE IN MY SHOES

You blame me, misunderstand me and then accuse,
But anyone of you, just walk a mile in my shoes
Would anyone of you been brave enough, to tread
The path I had to take?
No, not one of you, that is no mistake.
No one would have walked in my trouble and strife.
All this, because I loved, and was taken as a wife.
Trouble, it seems, has followed me all my days.
It has reached out, and touched me, in oh so many ways.
I did not want it, and God, all this I did not choose.
Yes, is there anyone out there, who would walk a mile
In my shoes?

Glenys Humphreys

SUMMER STORM

Hot, humid sticky
Grey skies now black
Thunder rolls,
Lightning flashes
The heavens open
Rain cascades,
Bouncing high
As myriad diamonds.
When lightning flashes
The darkness lifts
Rain stops
Sun peeps out
The world is now
A fresh sparkling green,
Leaves shimmer
Grass glistens
The world reborn
By the summer storm.

Glenys Humphreys

FEELINGS

Treasure the feelings
We both share today,
Hang on to them tightly
Or they may slip away.
They may start to go slowly,
Then in the twinkling of an eye,
We will be sitting alone
Remembering, then breathing a sigh.

Remembering the good things,
Of happiness shared,
The honesty between us
When our souls have been bared.
What was so beautiful
What was so right,
Has slipped through our fingers
Like dusk into night.

Glenys Humphreys

MY RIVER

How beautiful to me, is my river, the Dee
Wending its way calmly down to the sea.
Reflection so blue, by the clear cloudless sky
The slight swirl from the current, as it drifts on by.
When the tide is low, ribboned stretches of sand
Wind on for miles, like a soft velvet band.
But in only a few hours, how different the scene
Ominous, leaden, magnificent, moody and mean.

'I am the master, and I demand respect
Of mere human mortals, only I can protect.
I hold their lives, in the palm of my hand,
Only I can deliver them to the safety of land.'
This is what it seems to be saying to me . . .
No one can tame me, I'm meant to be free!
In all its differing moods, all the scenes that it plays
I would wish to gaze on it for the rest of my days.

Glenys Humphreys

A ROUND REMEMBERED

Bounding down to bungalows,
Leaping up the lane,
Pete-the-Milk and his lusty lads
Were 'on the round' again.

Windows rattled by clothes props
Woken out of bed
Mugs of tea and toast in the van
'Three pints there!' he said.

'Number four wants some more.'
'Six eggs for number ten.'
'Shut the gate at number eight
The dog'll be out again.'

In deepest snow, up Sandy Lane,
The milk would still get through
Along the Wern, at Christmas time,
Fresh cream and whisky too!

Goodwill to men, and milk for all
Hard work in early morn
But will the milkman still be there
Beyond Millennium's dawn?

Kath Williams

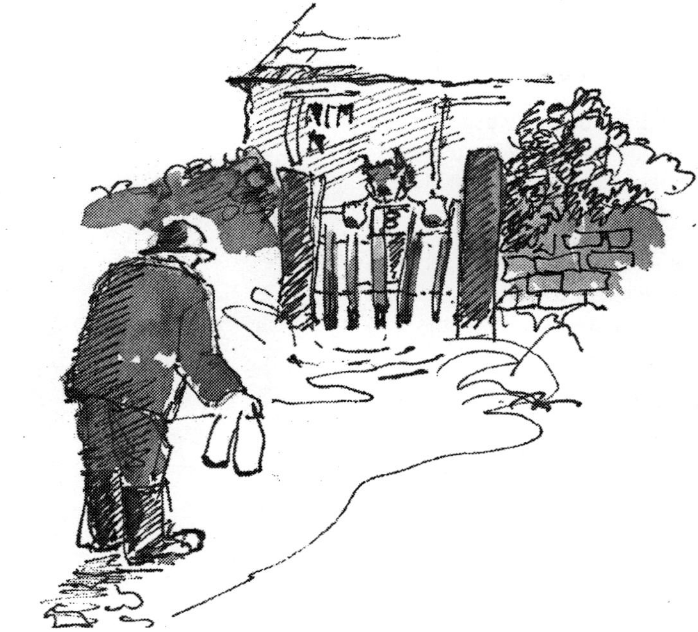

FACHWEN
Written after a trip with Ysgol Merllyn
to Fachwen, above Llanberris Snowdonia.

Once in this ruined shieling
When Dafydd was a lad
Where families earned their living
And times were mostly bad

The slag heaps as we see them now
Were black with slate and men
The lakeside was no scenic haunt
And warnings rang again

Great slabs of slate dismembered
The bowels of the hill
And lay in jagged mountains
For men to break, with skill

And Dafydd in his hillside croft
Would leave his wife each day
To craft the slate for people's roofs
A thousand miles away

But back home as she milked the cow
With beast and children fed
His wife would sing her favourite hymn
To thank God for their bread.

Kath Williams

WILLIAM RICHARD TOTTY
1909-1991

Those hands that guided horse and plough
And then so gently milked the cow,
They also gathered in the hay
To safely stack, at close of day.
The hands of William Totty

Through fields and meadows mostly hidden,
Bill plied his trade at Garreg Lydan.
From dawn 'til dusk, through storm and calm,
He tended his beloved farm.
The love of William Totty

His cheery smile, his kindly word,
The knowledge he so gladly shared.
He worked right up until the end,
Oh how I miss my dear old friend.
The friendship of William Totty

Norman Watson

OUR STREET

The street where I was born
Is now an avenue of fame,
Brought to notoriety
By the pen of Carla Lane.
She created Nellie Boswell
From somewhere deep inside
And around her built a family
To swell her breast with pride.

When I sit down to watch the show
My mind begins to roam,
It takes me back through all the years
To the street I still call home.
We lived just up from 'Grandad'
Number twenty on the door,
The house my family lived in
For forty years or more.

We had a neighbour just like Nellie
So strong and full of heart,
But none that I remember
She could have called 'A tart!'
All the men were working then
Not like it is today,
And not one single motor car,
Our street was safe to play.

The house that's now so famous
And bringing so much joy,
Is where the Goldsteins used to live
When I was just a boy.
They nearly lost their father
When his merchant ship was sunk,
On that fateful evening
Arthur never made it to his bunk.

He was homeward bound from Durban
In October thirty-nine,
His ship was called the 'Huntsman'
The pride of Harrison Line.
Caught in the South Atlantic
By the 'Admiral Graf Spee',
And then transferred to a prison ship
To take him on his way.

That prison ship the 'Altmark'
With Arthur still on board,
Finally dropped her anchor
In a Norwegian fiord.
It was there our men were rescued
From that hell beneath the hatch,
The Royal Navy came and boarded her,
The Germans had met their match.

With a street so full of memories
They dance around my head,
Things so long forgotten
Until the episodes of 'Bread'.
I remember the massive bonfire
For the ending of the war,
With an effigy of Hitler
Made by Jimmy Skidmore.

So next time you hear 'Grandad'
Shouting 'Where's me tea!'
Remember all those families
Who lived there, just like me.
There were Elliotts and Dongas
Clares and Skillicorns:
O'Learys, Aldags and Ablewhites
In that street, where I was born.

Norman Watson

BAGILLT ON DEE

Bagillt is a village
By a blue and restless sea.
Whose ancient roots reach far out
To the estuary of the Dee.
Where a million winter visitors
From the Arctic Tundra waste,
Twist and turn in unison
In such majestic haste.

Where fishing boats are lulled to sleep
To dream of tides to come,
And men will come from miles around
To work the Salmon Run.
As skylarks fill the air with sound
In their territorial flight,
Swift and martins twist and turn
To fill us with delight.
Whilst high above her sandy shores
In fields where cattle graze,
The distant views of England
Seem to float above the haze.

Norman Watson

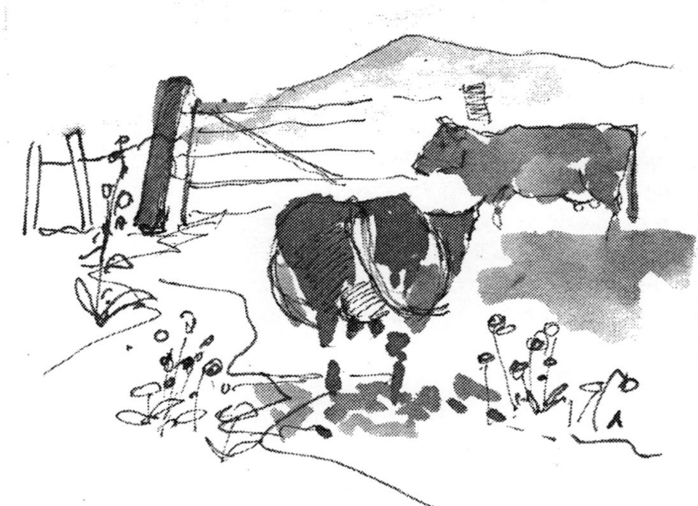

PROGRESS

Instant money, instant tea
Instant pleasure on TV.
Pot noodles and Cadbury's Smash,
A Hover mower for cutting grass.
Supermarkets for weekly shopping,
Fill up your trolley without even stopping.
Credit cards with which to pay,
Disposable nappies to throw away.

Coca Cola to rot your guts
People living in cardboard huts.
Dairy herds with Mad Cows Disease
And luminous sheep in our deep freeze.
GM crops to cause concern,
Will our leaders never learn.
I long for the days when time stood still,
With none of this *progress* to make us ill.

Norman Watson

COED BAGILLT
(Dedicated to Lisa and Gareth)

Walking through dappled woods
Nothing stirs
Except the stream moving,
Moving on its journey
To the Dee.
A silken thread running through
The green tapestry of life,
Woven by pine needles.
Wild garlic and cherry blossom,
The flowers of coltsfoot orphaned
And lonely,
Children laughing and splashing.

Asking and learning
I am also learning.

Norman Watson

OH I DO LIKE TO BE . . .

I'm sure it was very peaceful
Securely fastened in my chair.
My mother need never worry
For she knew I was always there.
Snug, content, happy in the sun.
At the seaside
When I was one.

I loved to build sandcastles.
But it was hard to say
When the tide would come rushing in,
To wash them all away.
I played in pools, caught fish alive
At the seaside
When I was five.

I know I thought I was too old.
Then the sand had no attraction.
To me the sea was out of bounds
And there never was much action.
Ice-cream cones were my choice then
At the seaside.
When I was ten.

A fluffy towel spread on the sand
Relaxing, turning, catch the sun.
Hoping the rays would not burn.
Being burnt was not much fun.
A need to be tanned when I'm seen
At the seaside
Aged seventeen.

Suddenly I was a mother.
Brushing sand from between wet toes,
Retrieving picnics from the sand.
Pacifying all the children's woes.
Loving all the things parents do
At the seaside
At thirty-two.

A deck chair on the promenade
With all past worries put aside.
Relaxing, enjoying the sounds
Of summer, husband at my side.
It's still the place I love to be
At the seaside
At seventy-three.

Joan Hough

DISILLUSIONMENT

Tell me more Dad, tell me more.
Did you play for the school team Dad
And did you always score
Or did you sometimes hit the post?
Or never get the ball
And did the others laugh at you
When all you did was fall?
Tell me more Dad, tell me more.

Tell me more Dad, tell me more.
Did you have lots of money Dad,
Or were you always poor?
Did your clothes have fancy names on,
Your trainers always right?
Or did you hide behind the shed Dad?
Keeping out of sight.
Tell me more Dad, tell me more.

Tell me more Dad, tell me more.
Did you always have your homework
And were you always sure
That as you went to school, your books
Were packed inside your bag,
Or did they throw them in the field?
Pretend it was a gag.
Tell me more Dad, tell me more.

I'll tell you more lad, I'll tell you more.
The teasing that you get through life,
You must learn to ignore.
Be proud of what you can achieve
And hold your head up high.
But tell me what you're feeling son.
The truth mind, never lie
That's the score lad, that's the score.

Joan Hough

LOVE IS . . .

Time hangs heavily.
People pass by.
Fingers strumming on the table
Just another day.
Unrecognisable food
Keeping me alive for longer.
I hear footsteps in the hall,
But no one comes.
White-coated figures
Dashing and flashing a smile
As if to a child.
My face is creased and dry.
My mouth is sometimes moist.
But on Wednesday he will come.
Kiss me on the cheek and say,
I love you Grandma.
Nothing else matters.

Joan Hough

LIFE AND DEATH

Those hands so small and fine
With eyes so clear and blue,
Life's first breath, so young and pure
A little world so new.
What will befall you in this life
What will your future make.
Will the wheel of fortune be at your side
Or will you have to fight
For every step and stride you take.
Who knows, for the path of life
Is long and wide, to worry is forlorn
So take that path with head held high
And keep the spirit born.

So trust in fate, for if you do
The world is there to see,
Enjoy your life, live it full
And hope for love like me.
For life is short, our time of death
We do not have a say
Just like our birth, life's first breath
That takes us on our way.
So death comes on silent wings
To whom we do not know
But when it comes, the angel sings
And tells us when to go.

David Watson

REGENERATION
(Written after the aborted demolition and subsequent restoration of the Old Chapel of Rest in New Brighton Cemetery Bagillt)

The warp and weft of our past
Forged in a pocket of profound serenity
In this small valley.

At its heart, structure threatened.
Its beat falters

Beneath the soil
There are . . . Steelmen and Mothers
            Spinners and Sailors
            Priests and Fishermen
            Daughters and Publicans

There is no difference now
Their bones feed the whispering trees
Their tears flow in the tumbling stream
Their voices are its murmur
Their singing, its birdsong.

Their disillusionment looks out
Through the eyes of their children
But their aspirations
Live in our hearts.

Nigel Ward Renshaw

TWO 'HAIKU' POEMS

Century dawning
Church bells peal out, pray for peace
The Millennium!

Fox flees to his earth
Badger sett-ward bound, cock crows
Sunrise. New day dawns!

Jacqueline Wilson

TO A GRIEVING MOTHER

Unwind his clinging fingers from your thumb -
To him at last that passive peace has come.
He takes with him the joy and trust you gave,
For you and him love stays beyond the grave.
No words or deeds will stay the power of pain
But true and strong you'll come to life again.

So softly sing your songs of sorrow
And send them soaring to the sky.
In time you'll reach a new tomorrow
And in your heart he'll never die.

Jacqueline Wilson

THE LADY IN THE WINDOW

Three days I saw her standing at her window,
It seemed that she was gazing time away.
At first around her candle-light would flicker
But then it faded, all was dull and grey.

I've wondered why she chose to stand there,
The view she faced was lonely and so still,
The lane was quiet, desolate, quite lifeless,
Not many climbed that steep and daunting hill.

Was she waiting, watching, for her future?
Perhaps she hoped her past she'd live again.
I never found the answers to those questions -
For suddenly she'd gone, with hope, I pray, not pain.

Jacqueline Wilson

DESECRATION

Four thousand years ago. Before Christ, before you, before me
On this same ridge they stood. Hard ground, dark stone
Now wrapped their infant son. In statue-cold serenity he lay.
Lost power of love, lost life. Entwined they stood alone.

Forever they would know his curling fingers
Forever in their hearts his gold smile lingers.

Two thousand years A.D. Stone Age man long gone.
We stand where once they stood. Ground churned, split wide
The power of scientific man reveals to hawking eyes
A tiny skull, small bones. Serenity is dug aside.

But forever they will see their infant boy
And forever feel no gold of sun, no joy.

Jacqueline Wilson

BETRAYAL

If you could feel the grief inside my heart,
If you could feel my tears upon your face,
Perhaps you would have found a gentler way
To leave me here.

Last night I read again the note you left,
The words you wrote to say that we had failed
To keep the fire of love between us glowing,
The fault was mine.

I thought I knew the way to foster love,
I held you in my heart with fierce pride,
But now I know my life will change forever
From this time on.

I have to try to ease you from my thoughts
I have to try to put away the hurt.
The future's mine, not ours, I'll learn. I'll learn
To let you go.

Jacqueline Wilson

CONTRASTS

I am white, pale, insignificant against you
Bold, black and beautiful. Black as ebony.
Black as the deepest depths of a starless night.
We are two contrasts as vast as the differences
In our birth places.
Distance once kept us apart.
You in your stark sun-baked continent
Mine the lush soft green-swathed gentle land.
No longer distant, our two colours mix,
Stirred by life, until many generations away,
We will be similar, in our contrasting motherlands.

Eryl Margaret

A MOMENT

Trees plunged in deepest cooling shade,
Edge the winding sunlit track
That leads through life's journey. Made
With trepidation, no turning back.
On-going, 'til a moment so sublime
With kindred spirit, side by side,
Enveloped in its beauteous sign
Of love, as if in heaven contrived.

Eryl Margaret

FISHY NONSENSE

How loud the catfish purred
As it swam the Coral Sea,
Past lines of praying monk fish
On their way to a monastery.

Deep in the ocean's depths
A kindly dog fish guards the plaice,
Trimming the anemones in the garden
Where butterfly fish's wings float like lace.

A four-eyed fish at the races
Watches seahorses chasing each other.
The blue shark is feeling despondent
He's gambled away all but his mother.

Cricket is the bat fish's favourite sport,
Playing in the sun fish's rosy glow.
Some young starfish make the most runs
Only because the old roach was so slow.

Cow fish and rooster fish are farmed
On a small holding owned by a brown trout,
Who takes longer holidays in Majorca
Going by flying fish to spend time being a lager lout.

The chub locking up at the end of each night
So the sea can rest and sleep,
Free of the roving lion fish
Driven crazily up the creek.

Eryl Margaret

HEN ARDAL BAGILLT

Wele'r hen ardal, du dy hanes,
Du gan fwg prysurdeb gwaith;
Ac mae'r olaf un ohonynt
Heddiw'n ddistaw dyma'r ffaith;
Nid oes neb o fewn yr ardal,
Neb ychwaith ar dir y byw,
Sydd yn cofio'r fath ddistawrwydd
Swn pob peiriant marw yw.

Nant y Moch a'r Gadlys hynod,
Lle bu toddi plwm cyn hyn,
Nifer lawer o hen byllau,
Olion rhair sydd ar bob bryn;
Waeth i mi heb ddechrau rhifo
Cyn ein geni ni bu rhain,
Tra mae hen aradr amser
Wedi cuddio'r oll â drain.

Tachweddfab (George Tattum)

Riverbank Smelting Works 1785

CYMRU
(This poem was found and presented by Carl Renshaw)

Hen wlad fy nhadau, gwlad dyffrynnoedd hardd,
Gwlad lle daioni yndd:
Hen wlad fy nhadau, gwlad sydd fawr ei braint,
Gwlad sydd yn enwog am ei saint.
Gwlad y cennin, gwlad y gerdd ar gân,
Hen wlad ardderchog ydyw Cymru lân.
Swn ei moliant esgyn tua'r nef,
Seinio wna ogonaint iddo Ef.

Hen wlad fy nhadau, gwlad y menyg gwyn,
Gwlad a'i haddoldai ar bob bryn.
Hen wlad fy nhadau, gwlad yr Ysgol Sul,
Gwlad sydd yn dysgu'r llwybr cul.
Gwlad y delyn, gwlad y gerdd ar gân
Gwlad ogoneddus ydyw Cymru lan
Swn ei moliant esgyn hyd y nef,
Seinio wna hosanna iddo Ef.

Hen wlad fy nhadau, gwlad y dwyfol air,
Gwlad y Gymanfa, ac nid ffair;
Hen wlad y pulpud, gwlad Pregethwyr yw,
Gwlad âi phobol, sydd yn ofni Duw.
Gwlad yr awen, gwlad y gerdd ar gân,
Hen wlad fendigaid ydyw Cymru lan,
Swn ei moliant esgyn hyd y nef,
Seinia haleliwia iddo Ef.

Cerdd yn hiraethu am Cymru gan
PTE. 34216 Samuel M Hughes (Sam y Glo)
9th BTN Yorkshire Regt/Italy 1918.

CADI HA

Cadi ha, Morris da,
Neidio tros y gafna.
Hwp! dene fo.
Cynffon buwch a chynffon llo,
A chynffon Rhisiart Parry'r go'.
Hwp! dene fo.
Fy ladal i a'i ladal o,
A'r ladal ges i fenthyg.
Hwp! dene fo.
Chynffon buwch a chynffon llo,
A chynffon Rhisiart Parry'r go'.
Hwp! dene fo.
Cynffon buwch a chynffon llo,
Hwp! dene fo.
D'wnsio i d'wnsio o,
D'wnsio am y penny o.
Hwp! dene fo.

Traditional

MRS ELLEN HUGHES (AUNTIE NELL) BAGILLT

(Gwraig, mam, nain a chymdoges dda)

O hirlwm daear i gorlan agos
    i'r Bugail Ei Hunan
    yr aeth, lle ni ddaw i'w rhan
    ennyd i flino'i hanion.

Norman Closs Parry

A tribute to Mrs Ellen Hughes
Of Wern Avenue who died 1997.

THOMAS PENNANT 1726-1798

Noble kin of pre-Darwin Days - who wrote
    reams on peasants always
He delved through their lands and ways
    being his own youth's byways

Norman Closs Parry

Bagillt Hall:
Thomas Pennant purchased
the Bagillt Hall Estate in 1766

NGH'LENNIG

Yng'lennig i yng'lennig i,
Blwyddyn Newydd Dda i chi,
Happy New Year, Christmas Box,
Mae mam yn ei 'sgidie,
Mae tad yn ei glogs,
Mae'r mochyn yn yr ardd,
Yn b'yta gwsgogs.

Traditional

Y DAWNSIO HAF

Y Dwnshia Ra Y Molista
Penny for a Dwnshia
A lickle-lee a lickle-lo
Oh ah a Dwnshia Ra

Traditional

*Sung by the children of Flint
and Bagillt in the last century*

THE BOOK OF LIFE

Life is like a living picture book
That gets older as the pages get thinner.
So don't waste the book
Look closely at the pictures
And turn the pages slowly
Because every book ends somewhere
And every line has to stop.
Every bush and tree and flower
Is part of the book.

Anni Watson (aged 8)

MY NAIN

My nain knows everyone in Bagillt and afar,
Come bus, train, taxi or car.
'Ta-ta Mrs Bennett,' the taxi drivers say
As they drive to and fro from Kwiks
On every shopping day.
'Alright Doris,' they call,
'Will we see you tonight, down the bingo hall?'
'Of course - how's your daughter,' she replies.
It's then you see the fear - in their eyes,
As they know she's going to chat for an hour, or two.
You'll find out everything about John, Bob, Sally or Sue.
All aside, no one likes to say goodbye,
Whether she's leaving the Post Office or the WI.

She's my nain, she's an aunt, a friend and a mother too,
So we all just want to say 'Thank you Doris';
But most of all, 'We love you.'

Rhiannon Bennett (aged 16)

SCHOOL SONG

Merllyn School is so great,
Be on time, don't be late!
Lots to see,
Lots to do,
Science, maths, and PE too!
The man-in-charge of this
Is no Tom, Dick, or Harry . . .
But Mr Norman Closs-Parry!

Jessica Roberts (aged 7)
(Ysgol Merllyn)

LAND OF MY FATHERS
(On seeing a photograph of a team of mowers in the Welsh hills at the turn of the 19th Century.)

Damp, cool, and misty
Grass and mountains,
Lonely road and lots of sky
Dark and bright and maybe some light.
Men may work so hard 'til night,
Let the men have some time too,
Freedom and life is meant to be.
No shops, no cities and little money,
So let their souls be happy and free.

Sarah Pugh and Rebecca Jordan
(Ysgol Merllyn)

THE HEDGEHOG

The lights flash, red and green.
Spines ready to roll up tight.
People walk up and down the street.
Noise all around.
Heart hammering.
People talk outside school.
Children shout goodbye.
Curled up but ready!
Cars stop . . .
Go . . .!

Sophie Williams (aged 7)
(Ysgol Merllyn)

THE ECLIPSE

Enchanting, amazing the sky full of sparks
Colourful skies and shadows so dark.
Light shimmering around the moon.
Interesting things to see but it will clear soon,
People laughing and shouting
So full of noise everywhere
Everyone still talking about it, here and there.

Katy James (aged 8)
(Ysgol Merllyn)

SPRING

Spring is the first season of the year,
When lambs are born and daffodils appear,
Days get warmer and nights get lighter,
Everything seems so much brighter.

Jade Jones (aged 10)
(Ysgol Merllyn)

SPORTS DAY (7/7/2000)

Sports day is coming,
Sports day is near,
It's the most exciting
Day of the year.

Everyone takes part,
Everyone runs smart,
We all shout Llywelyn
Go, go, go, Llywelyn

I hope I don't cause a drama
While my mum has got the camera,
I hope I don't fall over,
And be covered in green clover.

The scores for Glyndwr are 197,
The scores for Llywelyn are 211,
Yes Llywelyn have a victory,
Glyndwr are *History!*

Amy Horne (aged 11)
(Ysgol Glan Aber)

TOMATOES

Tomatoes are red
Violets are blue
This one's most
Ripe and aimed
Right at
    You!

Thomas Roberts (aged 11)
(Ysgol Glan Aber)

BUMPY LUMPS

I have a lot of lumps,
Which look like mumps.
I have a lot of lumps,
Bumpy lumps.

I have quite a lot of
Bumpy lumps.
Croaking frogs on big logs,
Make twitchy lumps.

I don't like the lumps
That make me itch all over.
They're so itchy and hairy
And big and red.

Thank heavens for cream,
To make them disappear.
At last they've gone!

(Next morning) Oh no.
Mum, where's that cream?

Carla Owen (aged 11)
(Ysgol Glan Aber)

WHY?

Just watch the toast while I go upstairs.
What?
Because the toast will burn.
What?
Do you want burnt toast?
What?
I will only be a minute.
What?
I only need to go and turn the tap off.
What?
Can you get the washing off the line?
What?
Your toast is burnt.
What?
I don't like my toast burnt?
So.
Can I make more toast?
So.
I'm buttering the toast.
So.
Do you want some?
So.
Will you stop saying so?
No.

Caroline Evans (aged 11)
(Ysgol Glan Aber)

THE HAUNTED HOUSE

Step in through the spooky gates
Be quiet as a mouse.
We're going to seek and take a peek
Inside the haunted house.

Ghosts are gliding along the hallway
Imps and spirits have pillow-fights
And catch you on the stairs.

In the kitchen there's a wizard
Making slug and spider pie,
For a very special Halloween surprise.

Upstairs in the dusty bedroom
Skeletons are getting dressed.
Vampires brush their hairy teeth
Werewolves brush their hair.
All spooks - must look their best.

Stephanie Wright (aged 10)
(Ysgol Glan Aber)

QUIET

We did it, lit the candles as you asked,
And Dunblane windows do not glow alone,
For we shall join you 'til the night has passed,
And heaven's Anniversary in the stars.

John Ovens

HOME FOR RETIRED GENTLEFOLK

The gilded clock tocked away the unimportant hours,
Whilst aged bodies dozed in a semi-circle of forced togetherness,
Autumn's half-light suspended dust over the old, old chairs,
And disinfected quietude mixed with the still, soft air.

Sepia photographs showed the orchestral violinist
Whose now arthritic fingers clasped her therapeutic knitting,
In rusted boned uselessness.

Logs flickered in the open fire, fastening its light upon
The resigned faces, like a silent film of long ago.
Stripped of the coin of dignity, submitting and paying for
The ticket on the platform for the journey out.

Rain slips respectfully upon the leaves within the grounds,
And Matron with her assorted warders treads the carpeted hall.
Soon will be arriving the waiting beneficiaries, who wish to
Interrupt last memories, take out of their miseries these
Station waiters from another time.

Healthy interrupters from day to day who will force physical
Life into surrendered limbs, painfully push on coats and hats,
And shuffle off towards the motor cars for forced fresh air,
To help elongate the brittle shell's existence in an
Alien world.

John Ovens

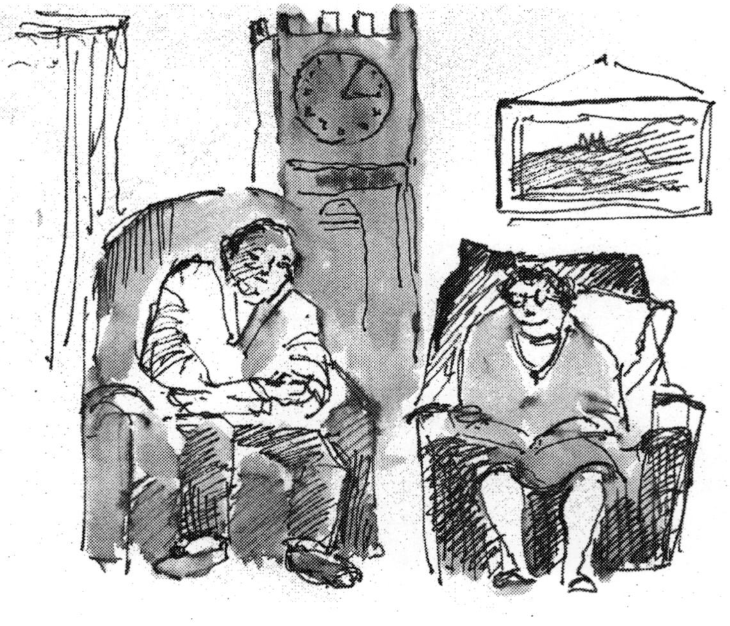

AUGUST EIGHTY-ONE - *JOHN OVENS*

He walked in the dark within himself,
And the dark hung black and low
For his heart was a part of his agony,
And that can no man show.
In flashes of light he saw the right
Of Helen's lonely Soul,
And reluctantly loved in a corner place,
In a diamond shining whole.

Chemistry flows where no sense goes,
And its cultivating scene
Is the curtain drawn on the coming dawn
And the crashing inland sea,
Floods over the mind with no escape
For the poor tormented soul.

He lifted the bricks in the daylight hours,
And humped the rubble, where
At the end of the day he took his pay,
And the Publican took his fare,
And Allan took the journey out
To the end of the night and day.

And Helen sat in the dim-lit bar,
Each evening waited there,
With a loving heart she became a part
Of the man who lost his way
Where the river runs by the Chemical works,
Where the trees bow heads of shame,
Where he walked his dog in the morning light,
Came the end of Allan's pain.

When the blue men came the choker chain
Had extracted the life you couldn't blame,
And those at fault with guilty shame,
Cried for the loss of Allan.

FOOD FOR THOUGHT

Quietly waiting for dinner, anticipating her expertise
With the roast turnips, a snippet of invention with the
Sauce peppered to titillate my tongue,
To go with the beautifully glazed carrots.
Why do I long for this, the mouth's practised tasting of
The red wine she chose, when once flamed loins
Are paralysed immobility. That isn't to say I'm dead,
But it is to say the young experience had such a
Warm gourmet tasting, when there was more magic
In the mind on a fish and chip evening and more
Bouquet in the vinegar and salt,
Than I can find anymore in your beautiful attempt
At replacement of my senses.
But I will raise my glass to your efforts,
And damn my memories with a large glass or port.

John Ovens

MY FRIEND

God's the beginning, God's the end,
God's within me, God's my friend.
The soul's lighthouse eternal spark
That shines within when all seems dark.
The vital force, the beating heart,
The one that throws the cupid's dart.

The long lifeline that takes my hand
And gently leaves on the sand,
To feel the sunshine on my face
And know the joy of love's sweet grace.
You lift me from the deepest sea
And breathe the breath that sets me free.

You are my home, my open door
My journey's end, my elvan shore.

Pamela Watson

THE DEE HORIZON

An Infinity of Tranquility.
Nothing out there, nothing beyond to perplex the solitude.
But.
A gentle never ending, neatly drawn line.
Creating and defining the sea's boundary from the sky.

Unpredictable, versatile, limitless, a force that
Won't be constrained by order.
No boundaries, no definitions will direct
The mighty Dee.

Your anger erupts into gentle waves of movement.
Whispers of your poignancy crash violently
Against the shore.
The wind hastens your fury and gives you the
Strength to break down the barrier and reunite you with
Your soul.

The night pressures the radiance of the pale pink sky
To gently sink to sleep in your arms.
Harmonious and serene, you intermingle graciously.

No boundaries will divorce you.
The imaginary line will never be.
While the passionate glow of the summer sky
Falls longingly into the Dee.

Danielle Rush

THE COMMUNAL HEART

We've nothing vast to offer you, no spectacles
To engross the mind's eye. Nothing expansive to
Stimulate the senses.

To look is to Deprivate the soul.
To feel is to Appreciate. To Realise
That the deceptively mundane marsh air, is pervaded
With intense weight of a
Deeper love.
An intimacy, too strong for the eye to behold.
Compassion which riddles the air, circulating
Through the Claustrophobic streets.

We've nothing vast to offer you, only a place where
Strangers are alien.
Where past is pivotal and
History secures Belonging.

Each man a link to an indestructible chain
Bonded, Solidarity. Togetherness.

Community
The heart of this empty shell.
Pumping blood with vitality, through the decaying streets,
Granting life to a village,
Which would be merely a shell, without its
Heart.

Danielle Rush

JUST ASKING

Tell me the words of the bird song
Sing me the tune of the breeze.
Tell me the joke of the chuckling stream,
Learn me the dance of the leaves.
Who plugs in the sun for the sun rays
Show me the path of a cloud.
Who shows the rivers which way to go
Why flowers have always bowed.
Tell me, who put the blue in the ocean
Who tinted the red in the sky,
Who sharpened the rocks in the cliff face
Who makes the night bird cry.

Tell me the reason for sadness
Who says we must suffer pain.
Tell me, I will listen, explain.
Then tell me all over again.
Who was the planner of misery
Who causes cities to burn.
Who plans the starving of the children,
All this I have yet to learn.

Vince Jones

BERGEN BELSEN

Oh yes I saw them friend
That cold alpine morning,
The walking dead, no semblance
Of humanity except shape and clothes.
Hideous clothes, patterned with stripes
And designs of various filth.
Twig thin fingers clutching rusty battered tins
In the hope some miracle with food would fill.
Then the dead, stacked like timber ready
To feed the fires of Hell
Oh yes I saw them.

Battle hardened men stood and cried
What to do, what to do?
Guards shot down with grim silent pleasure,
Little old children held gently in
Rough dirty hands of sobbing soldiers.
Yes I saw them friend.
I saw humanity at its finest
Yet again at its evil depraved worst.
I saw well fed warmly dressed town
Leaders, Mayor, Councillors, people of
High standing and men of the church holding
Handkerchiefs to their German noses because
The smell offended, but not to their
Eyes, because they had no tears.

I saw people smile and then die happy to be saved.
I saw others cower and scream, thinking
That we were the new tormentors.
Oh yes I saw them friend.

I went to hell, the Devil was not red
And had no tail or horns.
He was black, immaculate and soulless.
I went to hell without dying
But have died more than my daily quota
Each day since.
Oh yes I saw them friend.
And wish that I could forget the suffering
The bleeding, the resignation, the death
of *Bergen Belsen.*

Vince Jones

A LETTER HOME

My thoughts of you this night are deep,
When no one's near I tend to weep.
The daylight's fading as I write
My trench is dim - devoid of light.
How dank and cold this Holland ground
Battle damage all around.
Cries of pain and orders clear
Through the battle sounds we hear.

Taff and Albert went today
Without a sound they went away,
Albert from the Yorkshire Dales
Taff from Brecon, in South Wales.

I wonder Mam when it will end
It's so damned hard to lose a friend.
Strange to say I'm not afraid
My Will, my peace, both are made.
Have to go, we've got to pack
It may well be my last attack.
Should I not see the morning light
Remember me, our Mam -
         Goodnight.

__Vince Jones (3rd Monmouthshire BLA 1944)__

JUST OUT OF SIGHT

When you pass with quiet tread
With lowered voice beside my grave.
While you remembered who I was
Then I'm not dead

With every little thought you give
Of soldier boys who gave their best
And read my name upon the stone
Then I still live

When nature's green erases stain
Of war and carnage from the land,
My voice will speak in every breeze
Then I remain

Vince Jones (Belgium 1945)

INNERNESS

A nightingale with nought to sing
Like meadowlark with broken wing.
A flower when scent and colour dies
Of frowning clouds in summer skies.

                My sadness

A broken dream of someone dear
A sighing lute when none can hear.
The distant days beyond recall
Of whispering of the pine trees tall.

                My need

Though pass I through these wants and needs
The joy oft times these things exceed.
The balance of my moods will place
An even change - with nature's grace.

                My life

Vince Jones

LIFE'S CYCLE

We humans are like the buds on a tree,
Born to flourish in one season and three.
The Spring so fresh and vigorous in growth,
The Summer follows with leaves in full bloom,
We in our prime and life is in tune.
Autumn with its seasonal clime
Causes the leaves to change, in time.

> Winter arrives all too soon
> Shrivelled leaves in the gloom
> Leaves falling when winds blow,
> Trees denuded in frost and snow.

They represent friends from the day we are born,
We are filled with sorrow when we have cause to mourn.
Sadly we humans cannot outlast nature's almighty blast.
Thus severed from life's productive tower,
We enrich the earth beneath its bower.

Ceri Meese

MY GRANDA

I wish to write these verses Granda to release
You from my inner thoughts. To embalm you in
Words and memories of happy childhood days spent
In our humble homestead. You were a man of great
Stature, both physically and spiritually strong.
A respecter of God's word - loyal and hardworking.
You did not have an easy beginning, working down
The pit when but a little child.

You reared pigs, ducks and fowl so that we could
Enjoy a full table. You supplemented your meagre
Income by cultivating a prolific kitchen garden
With many fruit trees. You also painted rows of
Potatoes in Tyn Y Pistyll field, which were then
Harvested and hogged in the Autumn months.

I remember the day you brought home a tiny kitten
Called 'Fluff'. Harry Griffiths your friend from
Sandycroft who also worked on the railway 'Length'
Had given it to you for me. Fluff used to follow
You down the garden path, running ahead of you to
Scamper up the apple tree and wait for you to pass
On by then jump down and pass you again before
Climbing the next tree. This was repeated until
You reached your old wooden seat at the bottom of
The garden. As you sat on your seat in deep
Thought whilst smoking your pipe, Fluff would
Stretch up to your knees purring contentedly then
Frolic around you. What a picture of contentment.

Then what tragedy when you lost your dear wife Ann.
A woman of much strength and determination. For did
You not tell me that she had walked to Buckley and
Back in order to arrange for tiles to be delivered
For laying the kitchen floor. Then to lose your two
Sons, Evan Lloyd who died of typhoid whilst at the
Holywell High School and Seth Edwin, who at twenty-
Eight died on the 28th November 1918 following the
Influenza epidemic, after his service in the first
World War. Finally your devoted daughter Elizabeth
Ann who cared for you and your grandchildren, died
At the age of fifty-nine, after four days in hospital.

Your granddaughter Morfydd willingly took Mam's place
Giving up teaching to care for you in your advancing
Years. At home you were quite content to sit in your
Wooden armchair alongside the coal fire and smoke
Your clay or briar pipe. You enjoyed Sunday evenings
After chapel, when Mam played piano and Moll and I
Sang hymns before tucking into the rice pudding.
You lived by the Bible and died peacefully and
Gracefully at 88 years, in certain knowledge of
Your path to heaven.

Ceri Meese

MY CHOSEN ROAD

I was walking along my chosen road,
The road I've trod for many years past.
I stopped to rest my ageing limbs
On a seat worn smooth by storm and winds.
A youth came by and glanced my way,
'You're weary my friend,' he hastened to say.
'Aye, sure,' was my slow pensive response.
'I've well travelled this road that you now trounce.'

My path was strewn with love so rare,
Showered upon me by parents with care.
I've travelled alone through varying moods,
Passing persons I viewed of different moulds.

'How far will you walk today, my friend?'
'Oh! Not too far, just round the bend,
I'll take my time, I will not look back.
I've met good and bad walking this track.
Although you are young my kind young man,
You've a long way yet to seek and do.
I know not what lies beyond the bend.
I'll bide my time until journey's end.'

I pray the unseen will be just as pleasant
When I approach the last bend of the crescent.

Ceri Meese

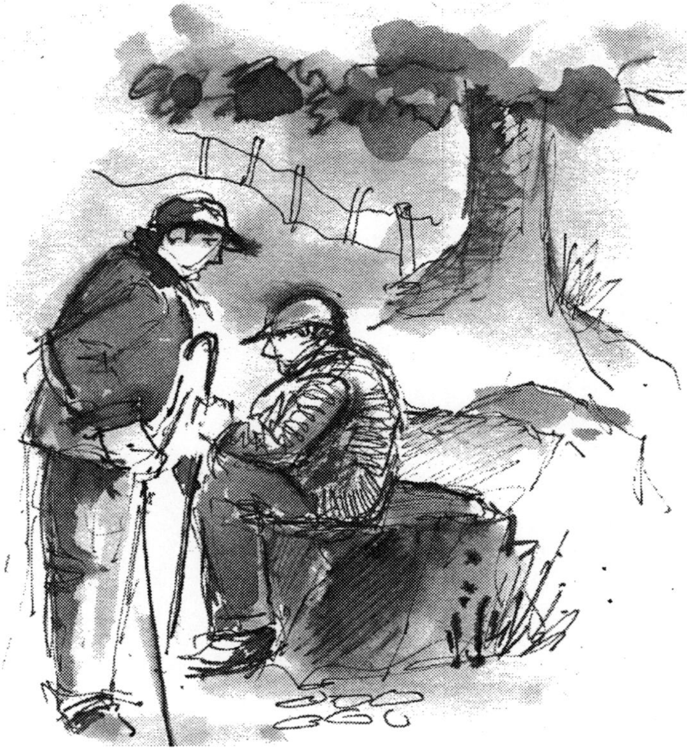

TRUST?
Written at the time of Iraq's invasion of Kuwait.

For if a man can trust no other
And they in turn can trust not him
Be they all so low in stature
Be their word no more than whim
Must we all look for the reason
Behind each word spoken clear
Beguiling sentences and phrases
Concealing truth from freedom's ear.

When the Tyrant sought to trespass
In a land not seeking woe
When the force of good spoke strong
Tyrant or truth, which was the foe?
For if they had but grown potatoes
Instead of being rich in oil
Would our troops have gone to battle
Invaders' ambition set to foil.

'Tis now time for all to ponder
Whether we be great or small
If our words be true with honour
Or are they just deception's call
For if a man can trust no other
And in turn they trust not him
What be the hope of Mankind's future
If the light of truth grows dim.

Barry Doleman

ODE TO BARRYMORE

There are no bars no chains of steel,
No dungeon deep no cage,
No sign of those who pass on by,
Of torment or of rage.
We see the smile the ready quip,
The joke which makes us laugh.
We see a man hold centre stage
But not his lonely path.

His tears they flow not outside,
But burn right to his soul.
A mask held only by his pride,
The actor plays his role.
For if a crack should e'er appear
And others see what lies inside,
It may well be they'd turn away
Conspiring to deride.
But come the day for all facade,
When it be torn away.
And great the man who stands his ground
And greets the new born day.

Barry Doleman

MY SHADOW

My shadow
Runs with me
On dry salty sand.
Wades with me
In shallow waters,
Skips with me
Through green mossy woods.
Dances with me
In warm summer fields.

It comes and goes with the sun
But isn't made of light.
It has no texture of its own
So borrows shape from earth and stone.

When I grow old
Will it stay young?
Will it run
When I must walk?
Will it dance
When I cannot?
Whatever happens
It is by my side,
From the day of my birth
To the day that I die.

Bridey Watson (aged 13)

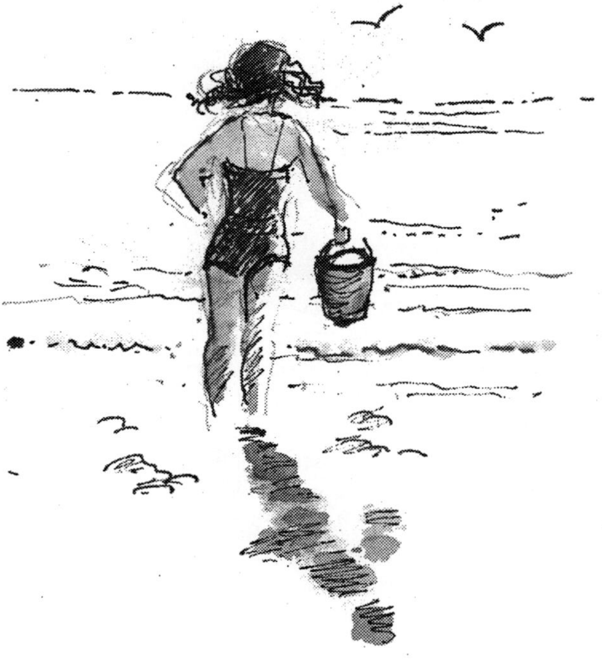

BAGILLT REFLECTIONS

The youth club was in the field adjacent
To the old Boot School. It was a large
Wooden shed, a place to meet, no decor,
Very basic. Luther taught the noble art
Of boxing whilst Winston just slugged it
Out. Peter kept himself busy building a
Canoe and ping-pong seemed so important.
It was a place so full of character, and
A meeting point for everyone. Maudie's
Sweet shop down the bank, quite close to
Mr Lloyd at P&O, Charas were parked up
At the ready, with tanks full of diesel
Waiting to go. Blackpool, Southport and
Trentham Gardens, the favourite day trip
Destinations then. The Red Lion and the
Royal Oak with Ike, a pipe tight between
His teeth. He was always laughing as I
Remember and was a very cheerful manager.
Mr Johnson the grocer up in his elevated
Shop opposite the cinema. With the Lone
Ranger and Tonto. Hopalong Cassidy with
The Cisco Kid. Flash Gordon was fighting
Against Emperor Ming with all his mighty
Forces. Then years later Peter Moore the
Most recent owner was fighting our legal
System for the many murders he committed.
Now residing in secure accommodation, at
Walton Prison. 'Involved', so to speak
With the Royal Family, *At her Majesty's
Pleasure* I think.

Brian Doleman

BEFORE MY TIME

Many years ago it's said
That miners worked in coal and lead
Digging deep below the shore
Raising buckets full galore
Far above by Totty's field
Men toiled hard with lead to yield
In dark tunnels lined with brick
Lots of ore to find and pick.
Just below - well in between
Different industries were seen
Some used hemp and others steel
Howells made the Laxey Wheel.

Through the village amble on
Pass the soldier from the Somme
Bagillt dock upon the Dee
St Mary's Church our legacy.
Keep on going move along
To the Tollgate at Voel Gron.
Gone too far, oh what a shame
A visit's due to Gadlys Lane
The Smithy and the Smelting House
Portray what Bagillt's all about.

Brian Doleman

OLD BAGILLT STATION

The old Bagillt Station! I remember it well
Imagine the stories both platforms could tell.
Steam driven Loco's a thing of the past,
The start of the Diesels that travelled so fast.
Passengers waiting to go down the line,
At Rhyl or Llandudno they had a great time.
Off to the fairground with 'kiss me quick' hat
But how Dr Beeching put an end to all that.

Brian Doleman

THE 'PARK'

Sewage eels, murky water and a stench
Beside our scenic coastal railway,
That carried passengers to the seaside.
Flood gates to stem the tide
Never ever worked in my time.
'Evans the Line' in control,
Sleeping in an old bomb hole.
Full of beer so appetising
Couldn't see the water rising.
Oops too late the damage is done.
Where has all the green grass gone?

Brian Doleman

THE ARMS OF CWM PENNANT

Oh, for the peace of Cwm Pennant
And the safety of mountains above,
Where the rivers and streams are like music
With a language of beauty and love.
Hear the distant call of the Raven
Soaring so high in the sky;
One day, at the end of my journey
My heart with the Ravens shall fly.

At rest in the arms of Cwm Pennant
I'll be part of the valley itself,
My bones will be part of the mountains
To share in their beauty and wealth.
Let my blood flow down with its rivers
On their journey to the sea,
But my heart will stay in Cwm Pennant
To fly with the Ravens: So free.

Then flying high over the valley
I can watch her breathing below,
From the first golden flush of springtime
Till she's covered, by a carpet of snow.
I have seeds growing in Cwm Pennant
And their beauty is starting to show;
On the wind I can hear their laughter
As off with the Ravens I go.

Norman Watson

THE BURNING ASH OF BROADOAKS WOOD

Broadoaks' high canopy glowed red
As sparks flew upward from the heat.
Below, from open wound she bled
To make a crimson carpet for her feet.
But still standing tall and proud
The great old ash withstood the pain,
Whilst around her friends cried out aloud
And a million tears put out the flames.
What should have been her funeral pyre
Instead became a beacon in the sky
Whose light will long outlive the fire
To show the world she would not die.

She stands there now, for all to see
Sentinel of Broadoaks, the old ash tree.

Norman Watson

*Vandals chopped into this old tree and
then poured petrol into the massive hole
before setting it on fire. Members of
Deeside Urban Wildlife Group contacted
the fire brigade who put out the fire
and saved the tree and the woodland . . .*

AUTUMN LOVE

Oh, what perfect wondrous bliss
Since tasting that first gentle kiss.
Instead of feeling winter's chill
I only feel the magic thrill.
No icy wind on fingertips
Just your warm breath upon my lips.
That burnished gold of autumn glow
Shall not succumb to winter's snow.

You've turned my autumn into spring
With feelings only love can bring:
You put the leaves back on the tree
And daffodils where only grass should be.

No more will autumn come and go
To be replaced with wind and snow.
Instead that tapestry of bronze and gold
Will live right on through all the cold,
Until at last, spring bursts on through:
Just like our love, to start anew.

Norman Watson

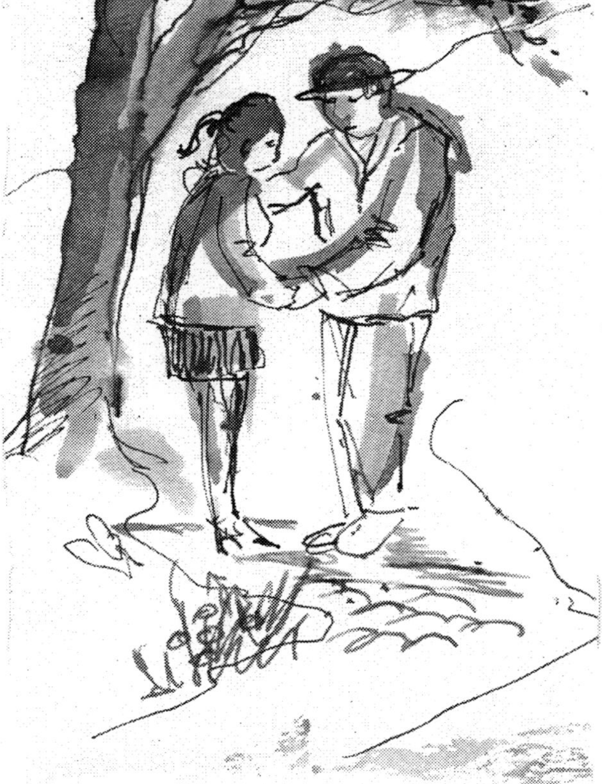

THE OWL

The Owl he sits on the branch and does stare
At the world around him, without e'er a care.
He sits and looks, like a wise old sage
Another day, another year, another book, another page.
The world dashes on, like the silly old Coots,
He just sits and stares, doesn't care 'Two Hoots'.

Glenys Humphreys

EBB AND FLOW

The flow of the river, clear, sometimes grey
Depicts our life, through the ages, day by day.
Some stretches, so calm, so tranquil and quiet
Flowing on into patches, tumbling, quick as a riot.
Then gently flowing in ripples that shine,
When our life is fulfilling, and heady as wine.

Now on into waters, calm, deep and green
Our moments of contemplation, our thoughts serene.
Oh so calm, like a mirror, reflecting scenes up above,
Showing us peace, hope, showing us love.
Gathering momentum, now angry, seething, bubbling.
Our times of depression, when we are worrying and troubling.
Then overnight, our worries are over and gone,
The river is calm and blue, reflecting the Sun.

Glenys Humphreys

CATERWAULING

Into the depths of my sleep, the torturous sound appears
Bringing nightmarish images, and heart-stopping fears.
Is it the cry of Satan's child, from the deepness of Hell,
Mourning his lack of soul? I cannot tell.
As my mind becomes alert, all my fears fall flat,
As I realise it's next door's bloody Tom Cat!

Glenys Humphreys

TWO OUNCES OF DOLLY MIXTURES

A cardboard frame with a folding door
Celluloid windows and a shiny floor.
Bottles of sweets, all in a line.
A painted counter and a sign
Says my sweet shop

The inch high scales with weights and pans
Just big enough for tiny hands.
Brown toffee pieces in a tin
Coloured papers to put them in.
At my sweet shop

Marshmallow circles pink and white
Chocolate drops that look just right.
Bright lollipops and dolly mixtures
Side by side in cardboard fixtures.
In my sweet shop

Paper pennies and circles of shiny tin
A draw that pings to put them in.
Three corner bags tied up with string.
I never tired of tidying
In my sweet shop

I love my shop, it makes me feel
So grown up, it could be real.
And when my silent friends have gone
I'll give myself a treat, just one
From my sweet shop.

Joan Hough

THE VEGGIE PARTY

The potato smooth and round,
Popped his eyes up from the ground,
Inviting all his veggie friends to tea.
Cabbages with curly heads
Came along in green and reds.
Two carrots and of course the humble pea.
The broccoli from his home
Called 'My hair will need a comb.'
The turnip brought his friend along, the swede.
The onion with his smelly head
Said the kidney beans were dead,
And the cauliflower had now gone off to seed.
The green beans growing tall
Always stood again the wall,
But pulled themselves away and formed a ring.
Mushroom wore his purple cap
And the sugar peas went snap,
And even Arti Choke began to sing.
So they danced the night away,
In their own peculiar way,
Till there wasn't any more that they could do.
When they'd taken off their skins
And thrown them in the bins,
They made themselves into a tasty stew.

Joan Hough

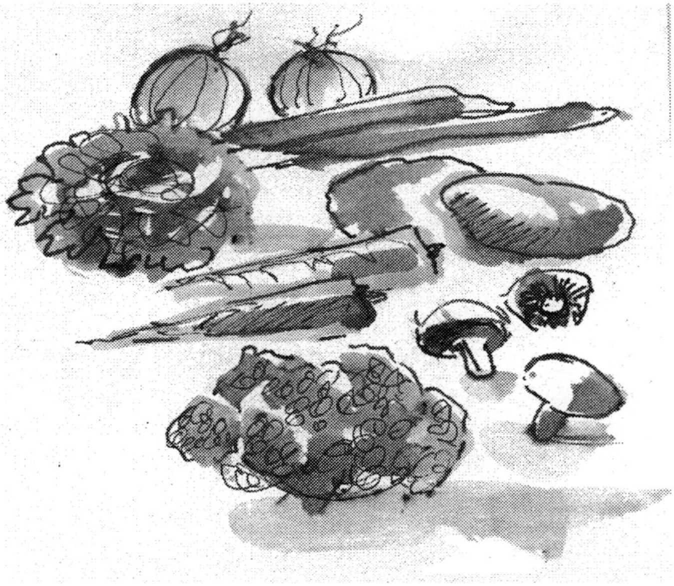

A MIST

In a mist of white satin
And rose petals,
We stood, our thoughts as one.
Love, contentment, laughter and tears
Of joy. All knowing.
Hopes and plans, without doubt.

Slowly, without perception,
Creeping into our minds as insects
Eat through spring leaves
Came indecision, torment
And overwhelming doubt.
Was it the end?

Where did it all go wrong?
Was it never meant to be?
Why the doubt, Jealousy?
Another love?
Now it has all gone
In a mist of paperwork.

Joan Hough

HAPPY DAYS

Our first love was the river
And that was plain to see,
We spent so may happy hours
In our trammels on the Dee.
Coming home weary every night
With our stockings damp and cold,
But we all thought it was worth it
When the fish we'd caught were sold.

Between each tide, our leisure time
Was spent around the Bar,
Talking of the fish we'd missed
And the dash back to the car.
The black mass in the gutter
That clung to our boots so dank,
The spies sent by the Riverboard
Who were lurking on the bank.

Oh yes they came from Chester
In their dark green mini vans,
Most times to be ignored,
Well they didn't have many fans.
Sitting on the foreshore
With glasses by their side
Watching all the fishing boats
Going up and down the tide.

They had purpose, that was fact
But bluntly speaking, they did lack tact.
Occasionally they made a 'kill'
To boost moral and give a thrill,
Eager hands to write reports
Important missions to the courts,
Barristers with lots to say
But no convictions here today.

Brian Doleman

THE 'HOLY WATERS'

From the deep lagoons in Milwr
To a gutter by the Dee
The Holy Waters tumble
On a journey to the sea
Over jagged rocks and boulders
In the darkest depths below
Cutting harshly through the mineral seams
With a never ending flow.

Constructed in the Great War years
To provide industrial need
The bricks brought from Ruabon
With utmost haste and speed
Local labour toiling daily
Many happy tales to tell
Whilst stealing all the water
From St Winefride's Holy Well.

Brian Doleman

THE CURSE

Stormin' Norman on his way
Walking down from Ffordd Y Dre,
Saw a farmer by the stream
With an earth moving machine.
His full intentions must have been
To level off the small ravine,
And further on the little wood
To be disposed of, if he could.

The wildlife that was living there,
No problem, he just didn't care.
The badgers, birds and all the trees
How insignificant were these.
So Norman got it in his head
This would not happen, so instead
He muttered threats with arms aloft
And somehow made the vehicle stop.
The man became an irate bloke
When he saw the tracks had broke.

Brian Doleman

'TUFTY'

He came along sometime ago
With a body oh so small,
Couldn't make a single sound
A squeak, well that was all.
I made a little house for him
Upon our kitchen floor,
But when we all got out of bed
We were greeted by the door.

Awaiting on the bottom shelf
For all of us to rise
A fluffy ball so full of fun
With true love in his eyes.
We were amazed and puzzled
How this puppy oh so small
Could climb up a wooden fence
That was over two feet tall.

We used to take him everywhere
On his own he would not stay,
Every single football match
Both home games and away.
Sometimes he really got involved
With players taking throws,
But went into retirement
When the ball bounced off his nose.

Both paperboy and postman
Were never liked at all
And anyone who rang the bell
Would drive him up the wall.
Letters were a favourite treat
Ideal to rip and shred,
A pint of milk left on the step
Just drove him off his head.

Now his body's getting old
Those limbs are not the same,
He struggles now to get around
With both front legs so lame.
Tottering down the garden lawn
Where he always used to run,
Chasing birds and rabbits
And having lots of fun.

Brian Doleman

THE ANTIQUES ROADSHOW

The Antiques Roadshow came to town
Hugh Scully's team of great renown,
Deeside Leisure was the place to be
For my Grandad's clock and me.
All polished up and clean
It was a Horologe supreme.
For the fifty years that he's been gone
My Grandad's clock, just carried on.

A windy day and bitter cold,
People queuing young and old.
Paintings, jugs and ornaments,
Receptacles for condiments.
An antique doll with painted lips,
A lady with some manuscripts.
The queue moves up a foot or two
People's faces turning blue.

At last we get inside the hall
I stand my clock against the wall.
It begins to tick and starts to chime,
I rush away - 'The clock's not mine!'
Hiding in the queue for porcelain
I finish up outside again.
By now my patience wearing thin,
I'm back outside, instead of in.

Porcelain went round the block,
Thank God I only brought the clock
And left that old Delft plate
That used to sit on Grandma's grate.
Back inside the hall once more
I thought I'll look around the floor,
People holding precious things,
A first edition, 'Lord of the Rings'.

Furniture took pride of place
Bureaus with such style and grace,
'Fit for a king,' I thought I heard,
'Ay, eighteenth century, George the Third.'
Laburnum, oak and ebony
Stacked up high for all to see,
John Bly was giving valuations
And pointing out the imitations.

Back to my clock in its mahogany case
With pediment carved and its lovely face.
Simon Bull is the expert here,
To tell me the make and also the year.
'Seventeen Sixty and made by Helm,
Quite well known throughout the realm.'
The value quoted came as a shock,
A mere fifty pounds for my Grandad's clock.

Then over at the painting stand
A distraught young lady needs a hand.
She sobs 'He's made a terrible mistake,
He says my Farquharson's a fake!'
His assessment was just one quick glance,
Which seemed to leave her in a trance.
She tells me then between the tears,
'It's been in my family for ninety years.'

'Highland Raiders' is a Work of Art
But maybe she didn't look the part,
With her old blue jeans and long blonde hair,
She said her father was a millionaire.
To be a star was not to be
But to go back home to obscurity.
A 'Highland Raid' of majestic might
In this Welsh border town, was put to flight.

Norman Watson

ROADSHOW BLUES
(To Norman)

The best part of the day for me,
Was going to Wales and Norman's for tea.
The time went so quickly, the tea went down fast,
Before I knew it the whole day had past.
But then arrived a piece of prose,
Which in my memory did close
That day; excitement, tension, cold
And disappointment when I was told.

And so I loved our Norman's verse
It seems the painting came off worse.
Value or note - 'tis back on display;
A plain wall lit, with sunkissed hay.
Whilst birds flock down 'neath sombre skies,
Contrasting shades light up their eyes
And gentle flowers amidst the corn,
Nod helpless heads before the storm.

How can such nature be 'just a fake'?
A story set in earth and clay,
Repeated, a whisper in canvas and oil,
Beauty enhanced through the labour and toil.
Just like the clock, now showing the strain,
An expressionless face as the day starts again,
Thinking, 'I'm only worth fifty quid, give or take,
I may as well be little more than a fake.'

A mere fifty pounds, or a priceless treasure
Who are these people who price up and measure?
The value of each lies deep in the heart,
Be it a clock, or a Work of Art.
Many years later, when I've passed away,
Perhaps my descendants will pause to say
'That old picture - it should come down,
The Antiques Roadshow is coming to town.'
And who will guess what they'll say it's worth,
Will serious faces break smiles of mirth,
Clasp hands together and whisper in glee
    'Farquharson! Last seen in 1903'

Liz Potter

THE FAMILY TREE

When my life has ebbed away
And suddenly it's judgement day,
I hope I've made some contribution
To go towards my retribution.
Perhaps something I've done or said
Will live long after I am dead,
To make the world a better place
Or disappear without a trace.
Just like the tree that's lived its span
Return to dust, where life began.
So when I'm gone, don't cry for me
I have descendants, like the tree.

And through our children life goes on,
Even when, we are dead and gone.

Norman Watson

FOUR WOMEN. THEIR STRENGTHS

Gold weighs heavy when formed
As a crown, upon a monarch's head.
To break new ground, be more aware,
Approachable to those who are served, give them serenity,
Her power is in her government.

A small piece of stony ground,
Seldom serenity there. The daily toil
To keep a home upon it, children fed.
Hair once gold, prematurely aged. Unerring.
Her power is in her love.

She stands her ground, and changes nothing,
When they don't understand.
But when they do, it is like gold,
Which brings its own serenity.
Her power is in her words.

In absolute serenity she lies.
Prostrate on the cold ground. Arms outstretched.
The shape of a living cross,
Bound to her God by a fine band of gold.
Her power is in her prayer.

Eryl Margaret

SHADOWS IN THE LIGHT

Soft whispers of a distant past
Echo within these lofty walls.
Such elegance may never be surpassed
And gentle solitude recalls
Sounds, of music soft and sweet.
Words that float beyond your dreams,
The gentle lap of waves beneath
The stony shore. In time secure.
So many figures, appear at night
Like shadows in the gloom.
Caught in their haste to write
A verse, a chart, compose in tune.
To weave their skills like cobwebs
Suspended in the glow of time,
And our imagination threads
With them, until our thoughts align.

Eryl Margaret

IT'S TUESDAY

Hurry up and get up quick,
Don't drift off to sleep again.
No time to eat or tea to sip,
It's Tuesday.

Clear the dishes from the sink,
Pick up the children's toys.
Time passes fast, no time to think.
It's Tuesday.

Smooth the sheets, shake the duvet,
Hang up all the towels neatly.
Plump the cushions, and polish the pouffe.
It's Tuesday.

Now all is tidy, clutter gone,
It's been a rush I know,
Just like a race that's to be won.
It's Tuesday.

He says he never looks inside,
But I'll never take the chance.
He just might peep. Now I've nothing to hide.
It's Tuesday.

The Window Cleaner's day!

Eryl Margaret

THE LAST PARADE

From the swirling mist they came
Silent ranks in fine array.
Heads held high in drill squad form
Marching to the realms of fame.
Disturbing not the morning dew
The ghostly army marches by,
Answering a soundless bugle call
To take their place for last review.

Their earthly shells in hasty grave
Are markers were they fought and died
In endless count across the land.
They gave their lives the world to save.
Of friends once known the ranks are made
And grey young faces show their peace.
As with soundless tread they advance,
Then in shadows slowly fade.

Vince Jones CPL 503
SWB Egypt 1943

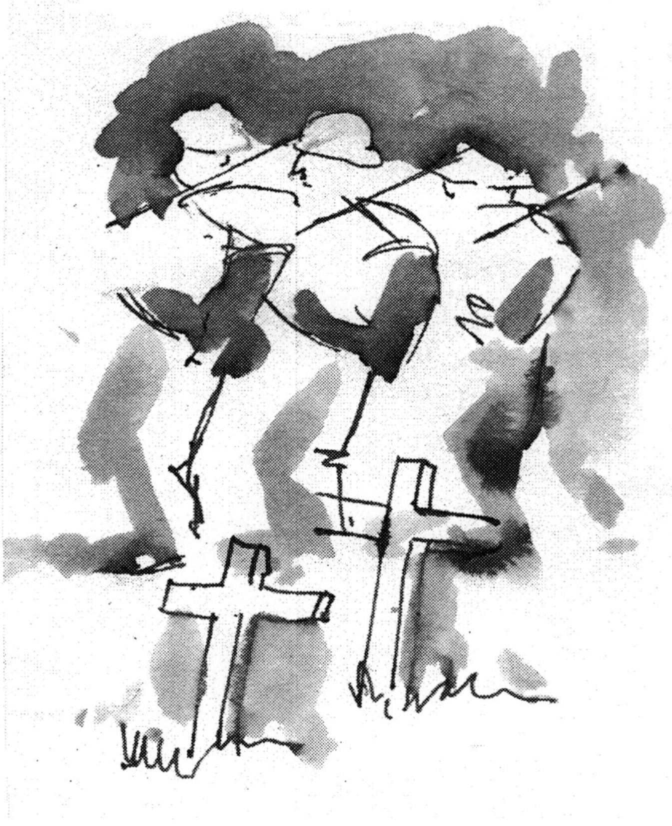

WALES

She towers above with rugged might
This fortress built by God not man.
A hearty people give her life
Amid the mountains capped with white.
A heavenly sculptor carved her dales
Her shoreline and her valleys fair.
A mighty craftsman planned her lakes
And ancient tribesmen named her Wales.

This land is nature's own domain
A picture that was given life
With palette of a beauteous tint.
The painter from a higher plane.
With angel choir with angel string
Of lute and harp, with God toned notes
With music from another world
The mountain dwellers learned to sing.

The fighting men of Wales are proud
Have left their mark in lands afar.
From shores of France to Zulu War
The Welshmen have not feared the shroud.
Though be it spring or winter long
Though strewn with flowers or abound with ice,
The voices of the Welsh shall rise
And fill this land of hills with song.

Vince Jones

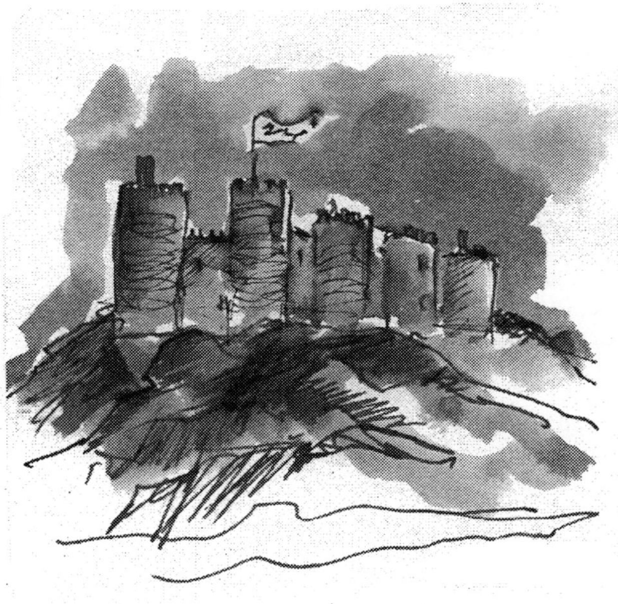

AFTER THE STRIKE

As she lazily gazed through the hazily glazed windows of the
Two litre Rover, she absently gloved the radio four and heard
The long strike was over.
And George of course lowered, the tone of the morning by
Protruding his horse teeth and sounding a warning,
'God Joan, 'twas a close run, a good job we closed ranks,
Good show the Express and the Sun, Mag's Army
Can be relied on to stick to their guns, and as you can see
The Christians have won.'

The Chapel that morning was silent in prayer, and mining men
Bowed to their Governing Chair, and with God on their side
Formed squads, with flags of the lodge on two poles,
They marched to the pit, first time for a year.
Welsh songs burst their breasts, but died on their lips,
Though they longed for a song they marched silently
On past the tips where the pickets no longer would be.

Don't push us too far boy, or else you will see,
Don't push us too far boy, or else you will see.

'Are you going to mother's?'
'Yes, will you see others?'
'Yes'
'What of the opposition?'
'There is none, old thing.'

And quietly, mining men's wives with their husbands and kids
To remember sang silently, 'Don't push us too far boy,
Or else you will see.'

'Those Welshies fought well, the Gordies did too,
We sequested their money and what did they do?
Formed communes and brotherhood's things . . . better dead . . .
                                                than red . . .

John Ovens

STRETCHING

I wish I was a painter, I wish I was a singer,
I wish I was a writer and I wish I'd made my marker.
But I guess I'm just a dreamer, so I'll listen to Celine
And I'll melt at Barbra Streisand, in the winter afternoon.

Why do we feel we have to, why the constant agitation,
A mind that cannot cogitate but bends the rules of reason.
I'm so thankful of the morning, of the challenge of the day,
But each evening, tot the whole thing up,
And see no greatness of the purpose, just the coldness
Of the season, and the losing of the way.

John Ovens

THE GREATER FRIEND

My all in life just seems bereft
That saddened mood draws nigh,
I've loved and lost I've nothing left
But memories that won't die.
Forsaken by a caring friend
'Twas no doubt fate to falter,
To trust to love and so depend
To find one's cares may alter.

Now in my moments of despair
I present and past regain,
My lone heart turns to silent prayer
While memories remain.
'Tis then I find my joys resumed
New hopes yet uncondemned,
For prayers can always be assumed
To find the greater friend.

William Harris

MEMORY GARDEN

We'll have a garden of memory
To ponder when in solitude.
The seeds we have planted so neatly
Have grown but will always include,
Something in which we have faltered.
Regrettable now it's too late,
Yesterday's works are unaltered.
The reminder is at memory's gate.

Planted are sins among sorrows
Smiles amid silence and tears,
Yet could there be brighter tomorrows
If today we would plan future years.
Can each little weed that may hinder
Be removed from the good things in time,
To burn as the coals to a cinder
And leave us a life quite sublime.
Memories are precious, to you and to me
So cherish your garden of sweet memory.

William Harris

List of subscribers

Meg Ainsworth, Foxhollows, Hatfield, Herts
Debbie Barnett, Marlow, Bucks
Doris Bennett, Riverbank, Bagillt
Ian Bennett, Llandegfan, Anglesey
Anne & Geoff Boam and Family, Bryn Madyn Hall, Bagillt
Ian N Brockley, Rhodfa Canol, Meliden, Denbigh
Brenda Bruce, Carmel, Holywell
Jacqueline & Christopher Bullock, Bagillt
Molly Busher, Riversdale, Brownsway, Holywell
Hugh & Irene Campbell, Edwin Drive, Flint
The '2 D's', Sandy Lane, Bagillt
Mair & Eric Catherall, New Brighton, Bagillt
Peter Carlyle, Bryn Gadlys Farm, Bagillt
Vera & Bill Coffey, Tholt Y Will, Caerwys
Pauline Couch, (nee Powell) Birmingham
Ray Cummins, Gadlys Lane, Bagillt
Mary Dale, Chewton Way, Highcliffe, Dorset
Jean Davies, Canon Drive, Bagillt
Lawrence (Nick) Davies, Manor Drive, Bagillt/Flint
Margaret Davies, (nee Price) Allt Y Plas, Pentre Halkyn
Jude Davis, Nant Gwynant, Gwynedd
Rita & Jim Dinsdale-Potter, Tan Y Glol, Lloc
John Doleman, Bryn Hawddgar, Clydach, Swansea
Margaret Doleman, Windermere, High Street, Bagillt
Jean Durham, ex Eldon Cottages, Bagillt
Emily Jayne Durham- Thorold, Riverbank, Bagillt
Jayne Durham, Riverbank, Bagillt
Kathleen Durkin, (nee Price) Cadr Idris, Glan Conway
Karen Ford, (nee Hughes) Banbury
Malcolm R Gleeson, Litherland, Liverpool
Andrew Griffiths, The Hawthorns, Merllyn Lane, Bagillt
Madge & Ron Hambley, Harborne, Birmingham
David Hanson MP, Cornist, Flint, Delyn
Harold G Harrison, Church Street, Flint

Elaine Hawkins (nee Hannaby) Ex Red Lion, Orchard Close, Shiplake, Henley On Thames
Agnes & Fred Holloway, Glan Y Dee, Whelstone, Bagillt
Clive & Darren Horne, Flintshire Glass Greenfield
Eryl & Frank Hudson, Bagillt
Alan Hughes, Glan Uchaf, High Street, Bagillt
Kathleen Hughes, Pen Y Maes, Treffynnon
Lisbeth Rowland-Hughes, Birch Hill, Llangollen
Winford Hughes, Deans Close, Bagillt
Andrew Humphreys, Neston View, Bagillt
Edryd Humphreys, Deans Close, Bagillt
Jane Humphreys, Mwrog Street, Ruthin
Jinny Humphreys, Highfield, Bagillt
John Humphreys, Wern Ucha, Bagillt
Robert Humphreys, Wern Ucha, Bagillt
Vi & Stewart Humphries, St Michaels Drive, Caerwys
Tracey & Alan James, Pen Y Glyn, Bagillt
Clifford Jones, Chester Road, Flint
Dora Jones, (nee Conway) ex Pen Y Bont, Hallfield Close, Flint
Frank W Jones, Fishpool Farm, Walwen, Bagillt
Glenys Jones, (nee Hughes) Llyn Beuno, Holywell
Irene Jones, (nee Humphreys) Greenfield
Joyce & Eric Jones, Wincroft, Drury
Margaret Jones, (nee Humphreys) Greenfield
Megan Urwin Jones, Trinity Road, Greenfield
Roy Jones, (ex Wern) Maplin Way, Thorpe Bay, Essex
Ray Lambert, ex Liverpool FC, Hawarden
Betty Lee, Buckley, Flintshire
Terah Oldfield-Lloyd, Lindon, Tyddyn Mesham, Bagillt
Gillian Marlow, Ellesmere Port, Cheshire
Arleen Martin, (nee Rollinson) Bryn Huw, Gwernaffield
Norma Massey, (nee Lancelott) Maes Pennant
David McLean Ltd, Enterprise House, Aber Road, Flint
Dilys Mortlock, (nee Jones) Anglesey
Dolly & Jim Murray, Sealooms, Lower Heswall
Phyllis Nugent, (nee Avery) Riverbank, Bagillt
Wendy & Chris Owen, The Poplars, Bagillt

Ann Partridge, Pen Y Bryn, Flint
William Platt, Walwen Isaf, Bagillt
Jane & Ron Plummer, Tree Tops, Holywell
Olwen & John de Prez, High Street, Bagillt
Edna Urwin Prichard (nee Williams) Riverbank, Bagillt
John Pritchard, Woodland Rise, Greenford, Middlesex
Frances & Stephen Pugh, Canon Drive, Bagillt
Ronald Pugh, Queens Avenue, Flint
Ken Radcliffe, Cae Haidd, Brynford, Holywell
Pauline Reece, Strand Park, Holywell
John Richards, Halkyn, Flintshire
Cicely Rieck (Cissie) Bryn Dyrys, Bagillt
Annice Richards, Walwen Isaf, Bagillt
Ann & Derek Randall, Bagillt Hall, Holywell
Anita Reid, Childer Thornton, Wirral
Mag & Nigel Ward-Renshaw, New Brighton, Bagillt
Doris Roberts, Llanelidan, Ruthin
Irene Roberts, Riverbank, Bagillt
John Roberts, Llanelidan, Ruthin
John Roberts, Halkyn, Flintshire
Ian Roberts, Ysgol Glan Aber, Bagillt
Joe Roberts, Dee View, Merllyn Lane, Bagillt
Gladys Roberts, Highfield, Bagillt
Gwyneth Roberts, Wentworth Avenue, Abergele, Conwy
Mair & Bernie Roberts, Sunnyside, Bagillt
Mary Roberts, (nee Carr) Upper Riverbank, Bagillt
Nicci Roberts, Cae Ffynnon, Bryntirion, Bagillt
Phoebe & Des Roberts, New Brighton Road, Bagillt
Shirley Salisbury, Pentre Halkyn, Flintshire
Irene Sayle, Brynford, Holywell
Ferol & Colin Sheen, Foel Gron, Bagillt
Jayne & Tom Spencer, Aston Clinton, Bucks
May Stanton, Bryn Dyrys, Bagillt
Beryl Stickland, (nee Morgan) Penhurst, Pen Y Maes, Holywell
Karen Tanner, Mostyn, Flintshire
Mary & Glyn Tattum, Meols, Wirral
Rev. Brian Taylor, Vicar of Bagillt

Dianne Thomas (nee Edwards) Flint
Ron Thomas, Riverbank, Bagillt
Vernon Thomas, Field House, Newbrighton, Bagillt
Alan & Megan Wall, Flint Mountain, Flint
Jean Watson, Gronant, Flintshire
Lenny Watson, Sunnyside, Bagillt
Dawn Westaway, (nee Bennett) Treuddyn
Barbara Williams, Bryn Maes, Llangunnor, Carmarthen
Gerald Williams, ex Pen Y Glyn, Bagillt
Gwladys Williams, Bod Erw, High Street, Bagillt
Jill & Ian Williams, Marlow, Bucks
Karen & Adrian Williams, Little Eaton, Derby
Kay Williams, (nee Thomas) ex Deva Cottage, Bagillt
Lily Williams, Richard Heights, Flint
Sandra & Craig Williams, Canon Drive, Bagillt
Shelley Williams, Greenacre Drive, Bagillt
Michael James Willis, Flough Road, Datchet, Berks
Lindsay Woodman, Tan Y Rhiw, Blaen Nantmor, Gwynedd